THE LIVING GOSPEL

Daily Devotions for Lent 2021

Theresa Rickard, O.P.

AVE MARIA PRESS AVE Notre Dame, Indiana

Theresa Rickard, O.P., is a Dominican Sister of Blauvelt, New York, a well-known retreat leader, and the president of RENEW International.

http://www.renewintl.org
Facebook: RENEWIntl
Twitter: @RENEWIntl

Founded in 1865, Ave Maria Press is a ministry of the United States Province of Holy Cross.

www.avemariapress.com

Paperback: ISBN-13 978-1-59471-997-4

E-book: ISBN-13 978-1-59471-998-1

Cover image "At the Foot of the Cross" © Jeni Butler.

Cover and text design by John R. Carson.

Printed and bound in the United States of America.

God has told you, O mortal, what is good;
and what does the LORD require of you
but to do justice, and to love kindness,
and to walk humbly with your God?

~Micah 6:8, *NRSV*

INTRODUCTION

A friend once shared this wisdom with me as I struggled to find God's will and way: "Terry, you are either on the way or in the way." Lent is an opportunity to get back on the way—to walk the sacred path. It is a time to review, refocus, and recommit to the way of Jesus.

St. Catherine, a Dominican laywoman, gives us instruction on how to walk the sacred path. She writes, "On two feet you must walk his way; on two wings you must fly to Heaven." Born in the sixteenth century, Catherine desired in her early years a life of solitude with Jesus, away from the noise and distractions of the world. As she matured, however, Jesus spoke to her heart the truth that would shape her entire life. How could she walk with only the "one leg" of love for God, if she did not walk also with the "second leg" of love for God's people? Just as a bird cannot fly with one wing, she could not truly love the unseen God without giving herself in love and service to her needy sister or brother whom she could see.

Lent is an invitation to walk more intentionally on the two feet of discipleship—love of God and love of neighbor. The point of entering these forty days of retreat with the universal Church—days of prayer, fasting, and generosity—is to live a more authentic Christian life long after Lent has passed. The call on Ash Wednesday is to "repent and believe in the Gospel." The heart of repentance is an acknowledgment of our failings and a resolve to change. Our belief in the Gospel is our hope in the mercy of God and the power of that mercy to transform our hearts.

This small book can help you reflect on where you are on the sacred path. Are you on the way or in the way? Are you walking with two feet—love of God and love of neighbor? What are the obstacles that keep tripping you up? How do you manage the bumps on the road? Who are the companions that help you to stay the course? Prayer and reflection on the daily readings can move you forward on the way of Jesus. Each two-page devotion for the days of Lent includes an invitation to prayer, a selection from the readings of the day, a brief reflection, and an action step encouraging you to connect your faith with your daily life.

I invite you to spend ten minutes with each day's devotion. It is helpful to develop a habit of prayer by choosing the same time and place to do so. I encourage you to use a Bible along with this book so that you can read the entire passage for that day. Citations for these are included each day under the heading "Listen." I find it helpful to begin my prayer with listening to a reflective song or instrumental music. It helps me to quiet my mind and settle my restless spirit. Perhaps this will help you too.

I pray that with God's power and through this devotional you will recommit to walking the sacred path with two feet: love of God and love of neighbor.

February 17
Ash Wednesday

Spend a minute or two in silence. Put your hand over your heart and listen for the Lord to call your name.

PRAY

Have mercy on me, O God, in your goodness; in the greatness of your compassion wipe out my offense.

~Psalm 51:3

LISTEN

Read Matthew 6:1–6, 16–18.

Take care not to perform righteous deeds in order that people may see them.

~Matthew 6:1

Walking the Sacred Path

A Vietnam veteran shared the story of the day his platoon searched a small village for the enemy Viet Cong. The soldiers tore the village apart and found no one, but they were ambushed while leaving the village. The young man was hit and awoke to find an elderly Vietnamese woman leaning over him. He dozed off with the thought that he was going to die. When he regained consciousness, the hole in his left side was cleaned and bandaged, and the woman was leaning over him offering him warm tea. A helicopter landed nearby to pick him up. The woman quietly got up and disappeared down the path.

In today's gospel passage, Jesus urges his followers to perform good deeds quietly and without thought of reward. In the first-century synagogue, this was a new approach. Jesus urges his followers to go even deeper—to purify their motives and to love freely. People who follow the way of Jesus are to do acts of mercy and seek nothing in return.

Today, we come forward once again to be marked with a cross of ashes—a public sign of our desire to walk on the sacred path of repentance and transformation, from the suffering of the Cross to the hope of the Resurrection. Ashes remind us of our mortality, our short and precious lives, and our need for repentance and forgiveness. These realities may make us uncomfortable, but they also have the potential to open us anew to the grace and mercy of God.

As you begin this Lenten journey, marked with ashes, choose spiritual practices that will move you along the sacred path of loving God and loving your neighbor. Do these practices quietly, freely, and, most importantly, with love.

ACT

I will review the three traditional practices of prayer, fasting, and almsgiving (acts of mercy or generosity) and intentionally chose a practice or practices for Lent that will help me to walk more faithfully on the way of Jesus.

PRAY

Lord Jesus, as I am marked with the sign of ashes, accompany me along the sacred path. Help me to choose Lenten practices that will help me to love you and my sisters and brothers more fully and freely. I entrust my Lenten journey into your hands. Amen.

FEBRUARY 18
THURSDAY AFTER ASH WEDNESDAY

BEGIN

Spend a minute or two in silence. Put your hand over your heart and listen for the Lord to call your name.

PRAY

I have set before you life and death, the blessing and the curse. Choose life, then, that you and your descendants may live.

~Deuteronomy 30:19

LISTEN

Read Luke 9:22–25.

If anyone wishes to come after me, he must deny himself and take up his cross daily and follow me.

~Luke 9:23

Choose Life, Follow Jesus Daily!

Fr. Tom Kleissler is the founder of RENEW, the organization I lead, and my mentor and friend. He is a man with a huge priestly heart, an inspiring and wide vision of the Church, and, most importantly, he walks the sacred path. The last few years, he has lived in the Dominican Sisters health-care facility. Because of his physical limitations, he spends most of his time in his small room. His body is fragile and bent over, but his bold and courageous spirit is still alive and well.

Fr. Tom chooses to follow Jesus daily in his present situation. He does not complain about his physical limitations and often tells me he is grateful to spend more time in prayer and spiritual reading. He continues to minister to a myriad of people through his ever-buzzing flip phone. He celebrates Mass and preaches once a week. He has made new friendships. He prays with the sisters when they are dying. Fr. Tom picks up his cross and chooses life daily.

The Gospels of Matthew, Luke, and John each state the three requirements for following Jesus: self-denial, embracing your cross, and imitating Christ's love. The Gospel of Luke includes the extra word "daily." This stipulation, "daily," reminds us that to follow Jesus is a daily choice, not a once-only choice or an only-on-Sunday choice.

We all have crosses that we don't choose; we only get to carry them with love and dignity. There are the obvious crosses of illness, caring for a sick loved one, grief, addiction, poverty. There are some less visible crosses: anxiety, depression, lack of self-worth, loneliness, unfulfilling work, confusion. Crosses can be redeeming when we take them up freely and carry them out of love. Each day, life and death are set before us. Choose life.

ACT

Without complaint or resentment, I will perform an ordinary act with love today.

PRAY

God of goodness and life, help me to pick up my cross and choose life daily. Give me a grateful heart, and when I am faced with negativity and adversity, let me choose the way of love. Amen.

February 19
Friday after Ash Wednesday

BEGIN

Spend a minute or two in silence. Put your hand over your heart and listen for the Lord to call your name.

PRAY

Have mercy on me, O God, in your goodness: in the greatness of your compassion wipe out my offense.

~Psalm 51:3

LISTEN

Read Isaiah 58: 1–9a.

This, rather is the fasting I wish. . . . Clothing the naked when you see them, and not turning your back on your own.

~Isaiah 58:6–7

No Fake Fasting

In a homily he gave at a morning Mass in the Casa Santa Marta, Pope Francis warned against "fake fasting." He asked, "Does my fast help others? If it does not, it's fake and inconsistent, and it takes you on a path to a double life, pretending to be a just Christian."

The pope has a way of using everyday language to get our attention. In the same homily, he said that as a child, he visited a friend's home and witnessed his friend's mother slapping their 81-year-old maid. Pope Francis never forgot that incident. He said that to give thanks to the Lord and, at the same time, treat others unjustly while they are forced to fast because they do not have enough to eat, is inconsistent and unchristian.

Fake fasting is concerned with impressing others. True fasting, rooted in prayer and charity, can transform us. Fasting can help us surrender to God whatever has undue power over us. It can help us to be more aware of the needs of others and chip away at our compulsions and distractions. True fasting leads to greater humility, awareness of the needs of others, and acts of mercy.

ACT

Today I will chose to fast from some food item and give the money I save to someone in need, or fast from my phone and spend that time in prayer or being more present to a friend in need.

PRAY

Lord Jesus, your Word is the only food that satisfies my hungry heart. Give me the grace to choose a true fast this Lent. Free me from my compulsions and distractions so that I may be more present to you and to those entrusted to my care. Amen.

FEBRUARY 20
SATURDAY AFTER ASH WEDNESDAY

BEGIN

Spend a minute or two in silence. Put your hand over your heart and listen for the Lord to call your name.

PRAY

Teach me your way, O LORD, your way that I may walk in your truth.

~Psalm 86:11

LISTEN

Read Luke 5:27–32.

I have not come to call the righteous to repentance but sinners.

~Luke 5:32

We are Made Worthy

When I ministered in a parish in the Bronx, I invited several parishioners to be extraordinary eucharistic ministers, to not only serve at Mass but, more importantly, to bring Communion to the sick and homebound. Thelma, a strong and faithful woman, was at the top of the class. She was rooted in God, prayerful, and had a great desire to serve. At a Sunday Mass, we had a commissioning ceremony for our new ministers, but Thelma never came forward when her name was called. She quietly left Mass after Communion. I worried she was ill or angry at me for something. I finally got her on the phone, and she reluctantly agreed to speak with me.

She poured out her heart, saying, "I'm not worthy to minister Communion. You don't know all the sins of my past. If you did, you wouldn't have chosen me." She began to detail the sins of her youth, but I then shared with her that really no one is worthy. Jesus makes us worthy and calls us to serve him, regardless of our pasts.

In Jesus' time, tax collectors were lumped together with thieves and robbers because of their perceived greed and collaboration with the Roman occupiers. Yet it was a tax collector whom Jesus called to be his disciple. Matthew was unworthy, a sinner, unclean according to Jewish purity laws, and likely collected more taxes than he was supposed to—Jesus knew all this. Yet Jesus said to him, "Follow me." Despite Matthew's past, despite everything, Jesus called Matthew. Despite Matthew's past, despite everything, Matthew followed.

Each one of us is called to follow Jesus' will and way. We are made worthy by his mercy and healed by his forgiveness. We cry out to God, "I am not worthy that you should enter under my roof, but only say the word and I shall be healed." Despite your past, despite everything, Jesus invites you, saying "Come follow me."

ACT

I will research a new volunteer opportunity to serve in my parish or neighborhood.

PRAY

Merciful God, give me the courage to say yes to your call to serve. Help me to know that I am made worthy by your love and mercy. Lord, I am not worthy that you should enter under my roof, but only say the word and I shall be healed. Amen.

Sunday, February 21

First Week of Lent

BEGIN

Spend a minute or two in silence. Put your hand over your heart and listen for the Lord to call your name.

PRAY

Your ways, O LORD, make known to me; teach me your paths.

~Psalm 25:4

LISTEN

Read Mark 1:12–15.

The Spirit drove Jesus out into the desert, and he remained in the desert for forty days, tempted by Satan. He was among wild beasts, and the angels ministered to him.

~Mark 1:12–13

Doing the Right Thing for the Right Reason

In Mark's brief account of Christ's temptation, he says simply that Jesus was driven into the desert by the Spirit and was tempted. We discover the details of the temptations in the longer versions found in the Gospels of Matthew and Luke. The three temptations are often identified as security, esteem, and power.

T. S. Elliot, in his play *Murder in the Cathedral*, examines a variation of these three temptations that every Christian disciple faces and adds a fourth. As the play opens, Thomas Becket, the archbishop of Canterbury, knows he must follow his conscience in the face of the demands of King Henry II, and Becket knows he will most likely be killed for opposing the king.

The fourth temptation is the most difficult for Becket—to invite martyrdom for the wrong reasons. Becket must wrestle with whether he is acting out of his personal desire for glory, to be remembered as a saint, or if opposing Henry is the right thing to do. Right before he is martyred, Becket reflects on the deep treachery of self-deception: "The last temptation is the greatest treason; to do the right thing for the wrong reason."

Jesus shows us the way by rejecting temptation and doing it for the right reason—to do God's will. We, too, say no to the temptations of the world for the right reason, for the sake of love—love of God and love of neighbor.

ACT

When I am faced with the temptation to do something unethical at work or unkind at home, I will examine my conscience and chose to do the right thing for the right reason.

PRAY

Gracious God, give me the wisdom and the courage to do the right thing. Purify my motives and help me to explore my conscience and offer a principled response when I am tempted to take the path of least resistance. Amen.

Monday, February 22
First Week of Lent

BEGIN

Spend a minute or two in silence. Put your hand over your heart and listen for the Lord to call your name.

PRAY

Let the words of my mouth and the thought of my heart find favor before you, O Lord, my rock and my redeemer.

~Psalm 19:15

LISTEN

Read Matthew 25:31–46.

For I was hungry and you gave me food, I was thirsty and you gave me drink, a stranger and you welcomed me.

~Matthew 25:35

Surprised by a Sheep

Fr. Abraham, a native of India, shared with me his first experience of leading a wake service in the United States. The pastor sent him to the funeral home with a ritual book, the address of the funeral home, and no information about the deceased man or his family. Abraham chose a generic scripture passage and proceeded to the funeral home, nervous and hoping he could be some comfort to the family.

As he entered the room, the deceased man's brother pulled him aside and asked if the Lions Club could conduct its service first. He explained that his brother was not a regular churchgoer but was a very committed Lion.

Abraham agreed and took a seat. He wondered what he could possibly say about a man who apparently was not a man of faith.

To Abraham's surprise, the three speakers talked about the inspiration that this man was to them. Each had a story about how the deceased man had volunteered at the local soup kitchen, how he had collected eyeglasses for the poor and elderly, and how he had done kind acts for his Lions Club brothers and their families.

Fr. Abraham changed the reading he prepared and chose today's gospel passage—the one about the sheep and the goats. Before the man's life unfolded through the stories of his friends, Abraham feared this man had been a "goat." Now, Abraham knew this man had been one of God's sheep. Abraham proclaimed the passage from the Gospel of Matthew and made the connection between the man's life and Jesus' word: "Whatever you did for one of these least brothers or sisters of mine, you did for me."

ACT

Today I will make a plan to perform a work of mercy this week.

PRAY

Loving God, root my life in the Corporal Works of Mercy. Help me to recognize Christ in the hungry, the poor, and the imprisoned. Amen.

TUESDAY, FEBRUARY 23
FIRST WEEK OF LENT

BEGIN

Spend a minute or two in silence. Put your hand over your heart and listen for the Lord to call your name.

PRAY

I sought the LORD, and he answered me and delivered me from all my fears.

~Psalm 34:5

LISTEN

Read Matthew 6:7–15.

Your Father knows what you need before you ask him.

~Matthew 6:8

Looking for God

In Elie Wiesel's book *Somewhere a Master: Hasidic Portraits and Legends,* he tells the story of a young boy who often ran away from Jewish school. One day the teacher followed him into the forest and heard the boy shout out to God the traditional Jewish Shema prayer: "Hear, O Israel! The Lord is our God. The Lord is one." The teacher was touched by the boy's action and told the boy's father. The father asked the boy, "Why are you wasting your time in the forest? Why do you go there?" The boy responded, "I am looking for God." The father replied, "Son, isn't God present everywhere?" The child replied, "Yes, but I am not."

Prayer is not about the right words or the amount of prayers we say. The heart of prayer is being in the presence of God. God is always present and our struggle, like that of the little boy in our story, is that we are not always present to God. Contemplative or silent prayer is a helpful way to embrace the presence of God. I struggle with silent prayer because I am often distracted. Sometimes, I consciously give the distraction to God and then let it go. Another technique I use is focusing on a word like "Jesus" or "peace" to bring my mind back to God's presence. I often pray the "Jesus prayer," which is popular in the Orthodox tradition: "Lord Jesus Christ, Son of God, have mercy on me."

Recently, at a retreat, the presenter invited us to quiet prayer. She instructed us to place our hands on our hearts and simply say, "Here I am Lord. I am present." If our minds started to wander, she said, "Simply say your name"—as a way of hearing God call us personally into his presence.

Spending time quietly in God's presence and listening to his voice in prayer will prepare us to be more attuned to God's presence in the ordinary moments of our days.

ACT

I will spend five minutes today in a quiet place and ask God for the grace to be aware of his presence.

PRAY

God, deepen my prayer life and help me to be more aware of your presence everywhere. Help me to pay attention to your "showings" as I wait in traffic, walk in nature, or look around my kitchen table. Amen.

WEDNESDAY, FEBRUARY 24
FIRST WEEK OF LENT

BEGIN

Spend a minute or two in silence. Put your hand over your heart and listen for the Lord to call your name.

PRAY

A clean heart create for me, O God, and a steadfast spirit renew within me.

~Psalm 51:12

LISTEN

Read Jonah 3:1–10.

The people of Nineveh believed God; they proclaimed a fast and all of them, great and small, put on a sackcloth.

~Jonah 3:4–5

Lent: A Forty-Day Challenge

Three years ago, I joined "The MAX Challenge," a fitness program that includes healthy eating, five days each week of cardio and strength training, motivational talks, and, most importantly, a community of people with the same goal and a desire to help each other reach that goal. The challenge starts with completing ten weeks of working toward your weight and fitness goals. After the ten weeks, you have a choice to make: Will you continue with the program beyond those fifty days and make it a part of your daily routine?

A few years before joining the MAX, I would start the new year with a resolution to lose ten pounds, then twenty-five. Like most people, by February, I was on my way to gaining back whatever I had lost. Becoming part of the MAX challenge was a transformative experience for me—transforming my mind, body, and spirit. I think it is working for me because of the daily 7:00 a.m. exercise with my group, support from the trainers, and an eating plan. One of the reasons the MAX works is that I am doing it with others. One of the surprises about the MAX is the strong sense of community—people helping people and working together for a common purpose.

In today's first reading, the people of Nineveh responded quickly to Jonah's message to turn from their sinful ways and get back on the sacred path. The scripture passage tells us that all, young and old together, fasted and were wearing sackcloth. They were transformed as a people—one helping another to get back on God's path now and into the future.

If you are struggling with keeping your Lenten promises, find someone to do it with you. Support each other and cheer one another on to become your best selves for God during this forty-day challenge and beyond. Restart today, and if you stumble, let another pick you up and start again.

ACT

I will ask a friend to help me keep up with my Lenten practice or find one to share with them.

PRAY

Loving God, give me the humility to reach out to another to assist me on my Lenten journey. Thank you for the gift of Christian community and for helping me to commit to being more engaged in my parish community. Amen.

Thursday, February 25
First Week of Lent

BEGIN

Spend a minute or two in silence. Put your hand over your heart and listen for the Lord to call your name.

PRAY

When I called you answered me; you built up strength within me.

~Psalm 138:3

LISTEN

Read Matthew 7:7–12.

Ask and it will be given to you; seek and you will find; knock and the door will be opened to you.

~Matthew 7:7

Knocking on the Door of Mercy

In his book *All Things Are Possible through Prayer*, Charles Allen tells the story of a man who each night before going to bed places his keys in one of his shoes. Each morning, he takes them out of his shoe and offers a prayer. His prayer simply asks God to help him remember every time he opens a door that there is a key to every situation and a solution to every problem: "May I never surrender to one of life's locked doors. Instead may I use the key on the key ring of prayer until I find the right key and the door will be opened."

During the Year of Mercy in 2015–2016, Pope Francis invited us to contemplate the notion of a holy door, "a Door of Mercy through which anyone who enters experiences the love of God who consoles, pardons, and instills hope." Knocking on the door of mercy is a Jewish expression for prayer. Prayer is a doorway into a relationship with our merciful God; no one is locked out. Thus, asking, seeking, and knocking are not three separate actions but instead three expressions of prayer.

In the gospel passage, Jesus encourages us to pray—to bring our needs to God. However, the purpose is not to inform or persuade God, but rather to express our relationship to God. We acknowledge our reliance on God and place our needs into God's hands. We entrust all to God's will. Prayer is the key to the door of mercy: cross the threshold and enter the presence of our waiting God.

Lent is a forty-day retreat and one of the Lenten practices is to pray not necessarily more but with a clearer focus on deepening our relationship with God. Prayer is knocking on the door of mercy and knowing God will open the door and sit with us. Prayer is entrusting to God all of life's situations, the closed doors we encounter, knowing that prayer is the key.

ACT

I will place my keys in one of my shoes before I go to bed tonight. When I wake up, I will take the keys out of the shoe, praying, "Lord, as I enter a door or doors today—crossing the threshold of my home, car, or office—make me aware that you are with me."

PRAY

Good and gracious God, I come into your presence knocking on the door of mercy. Deepen my relationship with you and help me to place my life in your hands. Amen.

FRIDAY, FEBRUARY 26
FIRST WEEK OF LENT

BEGIN

Spend a minute or two in silence. Put your hand over your heart and listen for the Lord to call your name.

PRAY

Out of the depths I cry to you, O LORD; LORD, hear my voice!

~Psalm 130:1

LISTEN

Read Matthew 5:20–26.

I say to you, whoever is angry with his brother will be liable to judgment.

~Matthew 5:22a

Feed the Good Wolf

There is an old Cherokee legend about a grandfather telling his grandson a story about two wolves. "A fight is going on inside me," he said. "It is a terrible fight between two wolves. One is evil—he is anger, envy, greed, arrogance, resentment, lies, and ego." He continued, "The other is good—he is joy, peace, love, hope, serenity, humility, kindness, empathy, generosity, truth, compassion, and faith. The wolves are fighting to the death." Wide-eyed, the boy asked his grandfather which wolf will win. The old Cherokee simply replied, "The one you feed."

On first hearing Jesus' teaching, it seems harsh. Is he really saying that being angry is the same as murder? No, but he does seem to be saying that we need to go deeper than checking off the box of each of the Ten Commandments. As followers of Jesus, we are called to go beyond obeying the rules of religion or civil law. We are to do the right thing with love and mercy—no looking for loopholes.

Anger is not a sin, but what we do with our anger can lead to sin. The longer we hold our anger, the more it can eat us up and destroy relationships. Anger is a normal human emotion, but unchecked anger can take control of our lives and hurt others. It can lead to broken relationships, loss of a job, divorce, domestic violence, and yes, even murder.

Both wolves live within us—the angry wolf, filled with retribution, and the merciful wolf filled with peace. Both try to dominate us. Today, choose to feed the good wolf.

ACT

Today I will name a resentment I am holding onto and try to take a small step toward letting it go.

PRAY

God of life and goodness, root out destructive anger from my spirit and fill me with peace, joy, and mercy. Give me the grace to let go of resentment so that my wounded spirit may be healed. Amen.

SATURDAY, FEBRUARY 27
FIRST WEEK OF LENT

BEGIN

Spend a minute or two in silence. Put your hand over your heart and listen for the Lord to call your name.

PRAY

Blessed are they who observe his decrees, who seek him with all their heart.

~Psalm 119:2

LISTEN

Read Matthew 5:43–48.

I say to you, love your enemies, and pray for those who persecute you.

~Matthew 5:44

Beware of Hate

Erica Chernofsky, a video journalist for the BBC, recorded the story of Max Eisen, an Auschwitz survivor. Max arrived at the death camp in 1944 at the age of fifteen. He is haunted by the memory of being separated at the camp "selection point" from his mother, who was carrying his baby sister in her arms and had his two little brothers in tow. Max has returned to the camp every year for the past two decades to tell his story. He joins the March of the Living, in memory of those forced on "death marches" from Auschwitz to the adjoining Birkenau camp. His message to the world is to respect each other no matter what color or religion you are. He has said, "I come back to tell people not to go down the road of hatred and intolerance. It is a warning. This place reminds you to beware of hate."

All religious traditions condemn hate as evil. But Jesus moves it to a new level—urging his followers to love their enemies. The teaching of Jesus offers an antidote to hate. He tells his disciples to pray for their enemies—to pray blessings on them. The love of one's enemies, that is, not the emotional feeling of love but the decision to forgive evildoers and perform kind acts for those who hate us, is the pinnacle of moral conscience. It evokes the highest form of love, and it mirrors divine love. In grasping the teaching of divine love, we touch the inner core of Jesus' message.

Hate produces more hate and can be as infectious as love. Beware of hate and choose love.

ACT

Today, I will create a prayer card for someone who has offended me and place the card in my usual prayer location to remind me to pray for that person.

PRAY

Merciful God, I pray for the grace not to harbor resentment against those who offend me or seek retribution if I am wronged, but rather to forgive my enemies and love them as you love me. Amen.

BEGIN

Spend a minute or two in silence. Put your hand over your heart and listen for the Lord to call your name.

PRAY

I will walk before the Lord in the land of the living.

~Psalm 116:9

LISTEN

Read Mark 9:2–10.

Jesus was transfigured before them, and his clothes became dazzling white, such as no fuller on earth could bleach them.

~Mark 9:2–3

A Transformative Moment

The famous musical *Man of La Mancha* tells the story of the ridiculed Don Quixote. He lives with the notion of being a knight of old and battles windmills that he imagines to be dragons. In one of the last scenes of the musical, Don Quixote is dying with his beloved Aldonza at his side. Aldonza is thought by others to be a worthless whore that Don Quixote idealized. He called her Dulcinea, "Sweet One," to the amusement of the townspeople and the scorn of Aldonza herself.

But Don Quixote has loved Aldonza in a way unlike anything she has ever experienced. When Don Quixote breathes his last, Aldonza begins to sing "The Impossible Dream." As the last echo of the song fades away, someone shouts to her, "Aldonza!" But she stands up proudly and proclaims, "My name is Dulcinea." For Aldonza, the moment of Don Quixote's death is a mountaintop experience—a transformative moment. The light of love enables her to see her true self—the Sweet One.

Jesus is transfigured in the presence of Peter, James, and John, and they are transformed by the radiance of Christ's love. They are no longer ordinary fishermen but have come to know their true selves and purpose— fishers of men and women and bearers of Christ's light to the world.

ACT

Today I will think of someone who loves me unconditionally and brings out the best in me; I will send that person a note or email expressing my gratitude.

PRAY

Lord God, open my heart to the dazzling light of your unconditional love for me. Send your Spirit upon me so that I can reflect your love and kindness to those I interact with each day. Amen.

Monday, March 1
Second Week of Lent

BEGIN

Spend a minute or two in silence. Put your hand over your heart and listen for the Lord to call your name.

PRAY

May your compassion quickly come to us, for we are brought very low.

~Psalm 79:8

LISTEN

Read Luke 6:36–38.

Be merciful, just as your Father is merciful.

~Luke 6:36

Forgive Anew

When Steven McDonald, a New York City police detective, was shot by an assailant, he became a permanent quadriplegic. Through a long process, he was able to forgive and even correspond with the young shooter. In his many talks on forgiveness, he used to say, "Every day I have to forgive again—and again. Every time I speak about what happened, I have to forgive anew."

Forgiveness is a process. It involves time, emotional struggle, and healing. As with any process, it takes a daily recommitment. Forgiveness happens when, through an act of love and God's grace, we can open our hearts toward the person who has offended us. A forgiving heart means we no longer hold others to their past wrongdoings. Forgiveness calls us to say no to the temptation to dredge up the past, rehash the story, and make another pay repeatedly. It is time to be freed of resentment, to move forward and live in a more peaceful way.

On the death of Detective McDonald, more than thirty years after he was paralyzed, it was reported that he had taken on "the stature of a larger-than-life symbol of forgiveness." His life was shaped as much by those three bullets that left him paralyzed as by the three words he famously expressed afterward: "I forgive him." After his injury, McDonald went on to be a public ambassador for his Catholic faith by speaking on the power of forgiveness and faith.

ACT

I will identify one person or situation in my life that calls out for forgiveness today and begin taking the steps that I need to forgive or to be forgiven.

PRAY

Jesus, our Savior, I praise you and give you thanks for your enduring love, mercy, and forgiveness. Warm my heart and help me on the journey toward forgiveness. Amen.

TUESDAY, MARCH 2
SECOND WEEK OF LENT

BEGIN

Spend a minute or two in silence. Put your hand over your heart and listen for the Lord to call your name.

PRAY

Wash yourselves clean! Put away your misdeed from before my eyes; cease doing evil; learn to do good.

~Isaiah 1:16–17

LISTEN

Read Matthew 23:1–12.

Whoever exalts himself will be humbled; but whoever humbles himself will be exalted.

~Matthew 23:12

A Floor-Scrubbing Priest

One Christmas, I invited my friend Fr. Abraham to join my family's Christmas dinner. I heard a big commotion in the kitchen and, when I entered the room, Abraham was on his hands and knees cleaning up the floor and reassuring my sister-in-law Lynn. Lynn is an incredible cook and hostess, but her worst fear had been realized. The beautiful and long-anticipated large prime rib had slid onto the floor, and the juices were everywhere. I wasn't surprised that Abraham was scrubbing the floor, but my family was shocked. They were used to the old days when our parish priest came to Sunday dinner. It was all way too formal, and he was gladly served first.

Yet that old experience should have been the shocking one. A priest, wearing an apron, with his sleeves rolled up, on all fours, pitching in to help my frazzled sister-in-law, and restoring the kitchen to order—isn't that an authentic image of a priest? The story of Fr. Abraham cleaning the floor has been told and retold—Abraham, the servant priest, is part of our family folklore.

Pope Francis has often spoken about the problem of clericalism, and one of the antidotes is for clergy, religious, and all ministers to "have the smell of their sheep"—just as on that Christmas day, Abraham took on the smell of a roast. However, this humble servitude is not only for first-century Jewish leaders or our own religious leaders but also for us. We all seek status and recognition, sometimes to the detriment of others. The words of Jesus are clear: be authentic, practice what you preach, and serve others.

ACT

I will do an ordinary job around my house or at someone else's house without being asked.

PRAY

Compassionate God, shape my life for service and set my feet on the path of justice. Give me a humble heart and serving hands. Amen.

WEDNESDAY, MARCH 3
SECOND WEEK OF LENT

BEGIN

Spend a minute or two in silence. Put your hand over your heart and listen for the Lord to call your name.

PRAY

My trust is in you, O Lord; I say, "You are my God."

~Psalm 31:15

LISTEN

Read Matthew 20:17–28.

The Son of Man did not come to be served but to serve and to give his life as a ransom for many.

~Matthew 20:28

You Be Jesus

Sr. Melannie Svoboda, in her book *In Steadfast Love*, shares a story about two brothers and their mom. Andrew, five, and Ryan, three, were sitting at the kitchen table waiting for their mom to prepare their pancakes. The boys began to fight over who would get the first one. Their mom decided to teach them a lesson. She said, "If Jesus was sitting here, he would say, 'Let my brother have the first pancake. I can wait.'" Andrew turned to his younger brother and said, "Ryan, you be Jesus."

We laugh knowing it isn't easy to be Jesus. We are selfish, yet we spend our lives as disciples trying to be selfless. Who wants to be a servant, slave, and—worst for me—to end up in second place? I want to win the trophy but, as we know, to win the race in Jesus' world is about serving, loving, and putting our needs last.

In today's gospel, the mother of two of the disciples asked that her sons sit at the right and left hands of Jesus when he entered his kingdom. Today, we might call her a "helicopter mom." The other disciples were angry at her request, and Jesus used the situation to teach them all a lesson: Can you drink the cup I am about to drink? If you want to be first, choose to be last; if you want to be great, be a servant. Today, choose to be Jesus.

ACT

Today I will perform an act of generosity and put the needs of another first.

PRAY

Loving God, give me the grace to put others first. Fill me with a generous spirit and a deep desire to serve others in your name. Amen.

THURSDAY, MARCH 4
SECOND WEEK OF LENT

BEGIN

Spend a minute or two in silence. Put your hand over your heart and listen for the Lord to call your name.

PRAY

Blessed are they who hope in the Lord.

~Refrain for the Responsorial Psalm

LISTEN

Read Luke 16:19–31.

And lying at his door was a poor man named Lazarus, covered with sores, who would gladly have eaten his fill of the scraps that fell from the rich man's table.

~Luke: 16:20–21

No One Ever Sees Me

In one of RENEW's *Be My Witness* videos, a man shares an experience that moved him to meet Christ through an encounter with a homeless man. When he was a college freshman, Sean's practice of bringing sandwiches to the homeless on the streets of Philadelphia allowed him to form relationships with some of the people he served. Each had a name, and each had a story that was often marked by mental illness and profound poverty.

The following semester, Sean was walking down the street and heard someone call his name from behind a planter and shrubs. It was George, one of his homeless friends, to whom he said, "Sorry, I didn't see you." The man remarked, "No one ever sees me." The words struck

Sean strongly and echoed in his mind and heart. Why don't we see the homeless? Why don't we recognize their humanity? Why don't we grasp that, except for the grace of God, we, too, could be homeless and living on the streets? Sean began to pray, "Lord, let me see you in the face of the poor."

Every day, when leaving his home, the rich man in today's gospel stepped over the poor man named Lazarus. It seems he didn't see Lazarus. Even the dogs in this parable come out better than the rich man. The rich man was probably not a bad guy, maybe just clueless—focused on himself and all his possessions.

In the busyness of our day, we often have our eyes on our phone and are not aware of the people or circumstances around us. Today's parable is a wake-up call. We work out our salvation in how we treat others in our everyday lives, especially those in poverty and the invisible. The parable teaches us that those who are deemed the lowest in society are, in the eyes of God, the most honored and beloved.

ACT

Today I will plan several meatless meals for this week and donate the money that I saved to a local food pantry or soup kitchen. Or, today, if I encounter a homeless person, I will look him or her in the face and acknowledge that person's presence with a simple greeting.

PRAY

Lord Jesus, open my eyes so I may see you in the face of those in poverty, the homeless, refugees and the suffering. Give me a heart full of compassion and empathy for my neighbor. Amen.

FRIDAY, MARCH 5
SECOND WEEK OF LENT

BEGIN

Spend a minute or two in silence. Put your hand over your heart and listen for the Lord to call your name.

PRAY

Remember the marvels the Lord has done.

~Psalm 105:5a

LISTEN

Read Genesis 37:3–4, 12–13, 17–28.

Israel loved Joseph best of all his sons. . . . When his brothers saw that their father loved him best of all sons, they hated him so much that they would not even greet him.

~Genesis 37:3–4

God's Dream for Us

The popular musical *Joseph and the Amazing Technicolor Dreamcoat* is a story based on the central character in today's reading from the book of Genesis. The musical version focuses on Joseph, the dreamer, and how his dream came true. In the beginning of the musical, the narrator encourages his hearers, initially children, to dream. The narrator says, "But all that I say can be told another way, in the story of a boy whose dream came true, and he could be you." It is a very entertaining version of the story but seems to leave out the action of God. We don't make our dreams for our lives come true by our own power or by chance.

In the biblical story, God acts in unobtrusive ways yet blesses Joseph at every turn. God is quietly present to Joseph through his trials and tribulations—when Joseph is abandoned and thrown into a pit and then sold to strangers by his brothers and sent off as a slave in a foreign land. As the story of Joseph takes its twists and turns, God eventually brings reconciliation and restores life and well-being to Joseph, his family, the Egyptians, and to Joseph's nation, Israel. The story is a witness to a God who uses even the evil plans of people to bring about good. Sinful actions do frustrate God's purposes in the world, but in the end, they do not stop them.

Joseph's dream was God's dream: for Joseph to be his best self for God, for his people, and for his world. God has a dream for each of us—to live life and live it to the fullest.

ACT

In the evening, I will review my day and reflect on a moment when I experienced God's action. I will offer him a prayer of thanks.

PRAY

Good and gracious God, thank you for calling me by name and accompanying me during the twists and turns of my life. I trust in your dream for me—to live a full and purpose-filled life. Amen.

SATURDAY, MARCH 6
SECOND WEEK OF LENT

BEGIN

Spend a minute or two in silence. Put your hand over your heart and listen for the Lord to call your name.

PRAY

Bless the LORD, O my soul, and forget not all his benefits. He pardons all your iniquities, he heals all your ills.

~Psalm 103:2–3

LISTEN

Read Luke 15:1–3, 11–32.

While he was still a long way off, his father caught sight of him, and was filled with compassion. He ran to his son, embraced him and kissed him.

~Luke 15:20

All Is Forgiven. I Love You. (Signed) Your Father

An article in *The Priest* (June 1999) told of a father and son in Spain who became estranged. The son left home and cut off contact. The father was grief-stricken. He searched for his son for a month to no avail. The father put an advertisement in the local newspaper. It read, "Dear Paco, Meet me in front of this newspaper's office on Saturday. All is forgiven. I love you. (Signed) Your father." On Saturday, 800 Pacos showed up looking for love, acceptance, and reconciliation with their fathers.

The father in the parable of the prodigal son runs to welcome his son home. He doesn't recount all the young man's past sins and how this son had hurt his family. The father doesn't make the boy sweat it out. He loves his son with a reckless and unconditional love. The father runs to him, sending the message, "All is forgiven. I love you."

God is like the father in this parable. God is reaching out to welcome us, to forgive our sins, to remove our guilt and shame. We are sometimes like the younger son who faces himself and his bad choices in the swine pen of his own making. The journey home into the heart of God and our true selves begins with a step away from sin and toward our God, who will rush to welcome us.

ACT

Today I will reflect on a person I am unable to forgive or a sin that is weighing me down. I will lay this burden at the feet of Jesus and pray for the grace to forgive and to be forgiven.

PRAY

Merciful God, immerse me in your unconditional love. Let me experience your mercy, so that I can share that mercy freely with others. Give me a forgiving heart. Amen.

SUNDAY, MARCH 7
THIRD WEEK OF LENT

BEGIN

Spend a minute or two in silence. Put your hand over your heart and listen for the Lord to call your name.

PRAY

The law of the LORD is perfect, refreshing the soul.

~Psalm 19:8

LISTEN

Read John 2:13–25.

Jesus said, "Take these out of here, and stop making my Father's house a marketplace." His disciples recalled the words of scripture, "Zeal for your house will consume me."

~John 2:16–17

Healing Our Church

In RENEW's small-group book *Healing Our Church*, each of the six sessions begins with the experience of a victim. One story is about Thomas, who was 16 when he was first sexually assaulted by a priest at his parish in New York. Thomas, who had joined the youth group in search of guidance, told the *New York Times* that the abuse continued for fourteen years until the priest died.

After revealing what the priest had done to him, Thomas left the Church. Despite his experience and his continuing doubts about clergy in general and the hierarchy of the Church, he later resumed attending Mass each week. He said that to allow the abuse inflicted on him to diminish his faith and his reception of the Eucharist would be to let evil win.

Courageous victims like Thomas, and laity and clergy who worked for many years supporting survivors, driving out abusers, urging the Church to accountability and transparency, have helped to cleanse the Church and restore it as a safe environment for God's children.

Jesus' zeal for God and the Temple impelled him to drive out the moneychangers from the Temple. He did not give up on the Temple and walk away but instead cleansed it and restored it to a house of prayer. Jesus' actions issued a radical challenge to the Temple leaders to face the scandal of their day. His action challenges us to condemn the current scandal of abuse and cover-ups, face it, and deal with it, and continue our baptismal mission to teach all nations, heal the sick, feed the poor, and comfort the forsaken. The Church can move forward from this time of darkness, but it needs all of us, the body of Christ, to work together.

ACT

Today I will pray for victims of sexual abuse and for renewed zeal to heal, restore, and reform our Church, working together with the clergy and bishops.

PRAY

Jesus, healer of every wound, I ask for purification and healing of our Church. I cry out for healing for the victims of abuse, for the lay faithful, and for our clergy. Infuse me with a zeal for our Church and a restoration of trust in our leaders. Help us work together as we find a way forward in hope. Amen.

MONDAY, MARCH 8
THIRD WEEK OF LENT

BEGIN

Spend a minute or two in silence. Put your hand over your heart and listen for the Lord to call your name.

PRAY

Send forth your light and your fidelity; they shall lead me on.

~Psalm 43:3

LISTEN

Read Luke 4:24–30.

Amen, I say to you, no prophet is accepted in his own native place.

~Luke 4:24

Jesus Run Out of Town

During his visit to the United States in 2015, Pope Francis addressed Congress but skipped lunch with the lawmakers to eat instead with homeless people. He shared lunch with 300 of the capital's less fortunate in a makeshift tent by St. Patrick's Catholic Church.

Following the example of Jesus, Pope Francis often chooses those on the margins of society over the rich and powerful. He also has been free in his critique of Vatican officials who bind others to the letter of the law but do not practice it themselves. He continually challenges all Catholics to be more welcoming and forgiving and less judgmental. He has entered dialogue with those of other faith traditions as well as with atheists and agnostics. This sometimes leads to people criticizing him and, worse yet, a small number wanting to drive him out of office.

In the incident described in today's gospel passage, Jesus runs into trouble with his fellow Jews, who find it difficult to imagine that God is healing people outside of Israel. They are angry and run him out of town.

Jesus proclaims that God's mercy and our care can be extended to nonbelievers and enemies. He reveals a God that shows unbiased love for all humankind. The Church is universal and cares for those beyond our borders, around the globe, and beyond our membership. The Church is not a club but rather a movement founded by and centered on Jesus Christ. As members of the Church, we receive no special treatment but are called as disciples of Jesus to show others special treatment—the outsider, the stranger, the foreigner.

God's love and inclusiveness is beyond any border we can imagine. God is not contained by language, geography, or religious differences. God's healing love flows toward all humankind and throughout creation.

ACT

I will identify someone who is often excluded from the group in my work or personal life; today, I will invite them to lunch or for a cup of coffee and be a conduit of God's preferential love.

PRAY

God of welcome, open my heart to the radical nature of your all-inclusive love and care for all people. I pray for persons and groups that I have walked past, judged, or failed to welcome. Fill me with your Spirit so that your love may flow through me as a conduit of your compassion, justice, and healing mercy. Amen.

TUESDAY, MARCH 9
THIRD WEEK OF LENT

BEGIN

Spend a minute or two in silence. Put your hand over your heart and listen for the Lord to call your name.

PRAY

Remember that your compassion, O LORD, and your kindness are from of old. In your kindness remember me, because of your goodness, O LORD.

~Psalm 25:6–7bc

LISTEN

Read Matthew 18:21–35.

Peter approached Jesus and asked him, "Lord, if my brother sins against me, how often must I forgive him? As many as seven times?" Jesus answered, "I say to you, not seven times but seventy-seven times."

~Matthew 18:21

Courtroom Forgiveness

In October of 2019, Amber Guyger, a former Dallas police officer, was sentenced to prison for killing her neighbor, Botham Jean. Guyger maintained that she had entered Jean's apartment by mistake, thinking it was her own, and shot him because she thought he was a burglar. According to an account in *USA Today*, Jean's brother, Brandt, asked the judge at the sentencing for permission to hug Guyger.

Brandt said that he wished Amber the best. "He showed with his grace and forgiveness how we should heal, and I hope people who are upset by the verdict will follow his example," defense attorney Toby Shook said. Jean's mother, Allison, commented that Brandt's gesture shouldn't be misinterpreted as the family "relinquishing responsibility." There is still a lot of work to be done by the Dallas Police Department, the Texas Rangers, and the city of Dallas, she said. Receiving forgiveness doesn't erase the harm you've done. We each need to take responsibility for our actions, understand the harm we have caused, make amends, and make sure it doesn't happen again.

Brandt Jean's extraordinary example of forgiveness helps us to see that Jesus' challenge to forgive beyond measure is possible. There is no justification for a "tit for tat" mindset. However, forgiving beyond measure doesn't mean forgetting, condoning, or excusing. It is about acknowledging the hurt, letting go, and becoming free of the anger and resentment.

The best way to learn to forgive the big harms is to work daily to forgive the small harms. Forgiveness is a daily choice.

ACT

I will think of a small hurt I experienced this week, acknowledge it, and pray for the grace to let it go.

PRAY

Healing God, I bring to you my wounded heart. Help me to acknowledge my hurt and my anger and free me from the burden of resentment. Immerse me in your forgiveness and give me the grace to choose to forgive daily. Amen.

WEDNESDAY, MARCH 10
THIRD WEEK OF LENT

BEGIN

Spend a minute or two in silence. Put your hand over your heart and listen for the Lord to call your name.

PRAY

Your words, Lord, are Spirit and life; you have the words of everlasting life.

~John 6:63c, 68c

LISTEN

Read Matthew 5:17–19.

Do not think that I have come to abolish the law or the prophets. I have come not to abolish but to fulfill.

~Matthew 5:17

A Blanket of Love

One of my friends, Terry Doyle, lives in Washington, DC, and met a young girl from rural Pennsylvania who has recently visited the capital. Hearing Terry's hometown mentioned, the six-year-old blurted out, "You live with lots of homeless people." The girl's mother explained that during the family's trip, her daughter was greatly moved by the sight of many homeless folks in the area. The young girl ran upstairs and brought Terry a fleece blanket and asked if she could bring it to a homeless person. Terry told the little girl, "My nun friend is visiting next week. We will deliver it."

When I arrived, Terry gave me my marching orders and we quickly identified a recipient for the gift. I approached a homeless man, told him about the concern of the little girl, and asked if he could use the blanket. He graciously accepted the gift. As I thanked him and began to walk away, he called after me, "God bless you and that little girl."

In today's gospel passage, we hear that Jesus did not come to abolish the Law but to fulfill it. This does not mean a mere continuation of the Law but rather the transcendence of it. Jesus, by his word and deeds, as recorded in the scriptures, announced mercy, justice, and love as the weightier matters of the Law, the standards by which the whole Law must be judged. For Jesus, to obey the Law was not to scrupulously follow its letter but rather to abide by its spirit. Jesus fulfilled the law of God by becoming God's loving presence in the world and offering his life for our salvation.

As Jesus' disciples, we too are called to reveal God by our acts of love—without judgment or conditions. The little girl, offering a blanket for a homeless man, and my friend Terry's willingness to help was a fulfillment of God's law of love and mercy.

ACT

Today I will do an act of kindness that reflects the Great Commandment—to love God with your whole heart and your neighbor as yourself.

PRAY

Loving God, help me to obey your law in the spirit of mercy, justice, and love. Infuse in me a new spirit today as I struggle to choose to follow your will. Jesus, have mercy on me. Amen.

THURSDAY, MARCH 11
THIRD WEEK OF LENT

BEGIN

Spend a minute or two in silence. Put your hand over your heart and listen for the Lord to call your name.

PRAY

Oh, that today you would hear his voice: "Harden not your hearts."

~Psalm 95:7d–8a

LISTEN

Read Luke 11:14–23.

Every kingdom divided against itself will be laid waste and house will fall against house.

~Luke 11:17

House Divided

In 1858, US Senate candidate Abraham Lincoln delivered what has been known ever since as the House Divided speech. Lincoln argued that the current situation of slavery legalized in some states and outlawed in others was untenable, that America could not continue this divided path. "A house divided against itself cannot stand," he said, using words drawn from today's gospel passage and also found in the Gospels of Matthew and Mark. The reference to the Bible would have been familiar to his audience. Lincoln was right; in 1861, a bloody civil war began.

Although there is no single issue that geographically and economically divides our country in the way slavery did, we do find ourselves sharply divided. The polarization around politics has seeped into the Church. The lack of respect, finger pointing, and insults may not cause us to fall but they do make it difficult to stand erect.

Pope Francis in a general audience in Vatican City encouraged Catholics to give up "insults" on social media for Lent. He said, "We live in an atmosphere polluted by too much verbal violence, too many offensive and harmful words, which are amplified by the internet." Francis knows that only by standing together can we move forward in hope as a Church and bring the Good News of Jesus Christ to our world. He encourages us to embrace "synodality"—the call to enter freely and respectfully into sacred conversations with laity, clergy, and bishops as the body of Christ for the sake of hearing the voice of the Spirit. First and foremost, we are Catholic, and as a Church we are not beholden to an ideology. We don't worship an idea but a person—the person of Jesus Christ.

ACT

Today I will avoid posting or reading social media trash-talk and refrain from trashing someone who has a different viewpoint on politics or the Church.

PRAY

Come Holy Spirit, open my heart to love and my ears to listen to those of different viewpoints. Give me a humble spirit and help me to be a peacemaker in union with you and the whole Church. Amen.

FRIDAY, MARCH 12
THIRD WEEK OF LENT

BEGIN

Spend a minute or two in silence. Put your hand over your heart and listen for the Lord to call your name.

PRAY

If only my people would hear me, and Israel walk in my ways, I would feed them with the best of wheat, and with honey from the rock I would fill them.

~Psalm 81:14, 17

LISTEN

Read Mark 12:28–34.

You shall love the Lord your God with all your heart, with all your soul, with all your mind, and with all your strength.

~Mark 12:30

Bringing God into Our Homes

One Christmas, my friend Jude, a Dominican priest, gave me an unusual gift—a mezuzah. This small case contains a piece of parchment inscribed with verses of the Hebrew Scriptures, including the Shema prayer. The Shema prayer is taken from Deuteronomy 6:4–9, and it is summed up in today's gospel reading in Jesus' identification of the Greatest Commandment: the Shema prayer declares the oneness of God and the call to love God and neighbor with all our hearts. Jews continue to pray this prayer every morning and evening, and they affix the mezuzah to the doorposts of their homes as a reminder to live faith in their daily life.

As Dominicans, known as "the order of preachers," Jude and I share a passion for the Word of God. Although hanging a mezuzah is a Jewish custom, I was delighted to affix the mezuzah to the doorpost of my bedroom as a sign of my love for God's Word and a reminder to live that Word daily by loving God and my neighbor.

Catholics also have a tradition of placing religious symbols in our homes as a sign of our faith. When I was growing up, my home had a crucifix in every bedroom, a picture of the Sacred Heart in the kitchen, and a statue of Mary in my parents' bedroom. Yet in many Anglo-Catholic homes now, symbols of the faith are no longer present.

These signs can remind us to invite God into our daily lives and be a testimony to our faith, as well as invite conversations with others who may be seeking faith. I think tangible signs of faith are particularly important to our children and grandchildren. I give religious gifts to my nieces and nephews for special occasions, usually a crucifix for weddings and a holy-water font for the baptism of their children. A home ought to be a domestic church—a tangible sign of God's presence among us.

ACT

Today I will hang a crucifix or another symbol of the Catholic faith somewhere in my home.

PRAY

Hear, O people, the Lord is one. Loving God, give me a single-hearted devotion to you and a generous love of my neighbor. Help me to bring signs of your presence into my home and into the homes of those I love. Amen.

SATURDAY, MARCH 13
THIRD WEEK OF LENT

BEGIN

Spend a minute or two in silence. Put your hand over your heart and listen for the Lord to call your name.

PRAY

A heart contrite and humbled O God, you will not spurn.

~Psalm 51:19

LISTEN

Read Luke 18:9–14.

The tax collector stood off at a distance and would not even raise his eyes to heaven but beat his breast and prayed, "O God, be merciful to me a sinner."

~Luke 18:13

I Am So Worthy

A priest once shared a story about when he was a seminarian and worked hard at being holy. For Lent, Joe decided that every Friday he would do a total fast and drink only water that day. In the seminary, there was one fellow seminarian that really bothered him. This guy was loud, was late for prayers, and never seemed to take life seriously. One Friday during Lent, Joe heard laughing from the dining room. As he peered in, there was this guy telling jokes, eating pizza, and drinking a beer—during Lent! Fasting Joe was glad he wasn't like that seminarian.

After the Easter Vigil, Joe lingered in the chapel, feeling very pleased with himself. He said, "I was thinking,

O Lord I am so worthy. . . ." On Easter morning, the seminary was clearing out. Joe went to answer the doorbell. There was a homeless man looking for a priest who often helped him. Joe told the man the priest had gone home, the seminary was closed, and Joe went to his room to pack. As he left with his suitcase, he heard noise from the priests' dining room. He looked in and found that loud seminarian and the homeless man, talking and eating together. Joe slammed the door and walked away angry, thinking to himself, *They should not be in there; the seminary is closed!* As he drove around the neighborhood, his anger slowly dissipated. Joe realized the loud seminarian's willingness to share Christ with the homeless man was more impactful than all of his self-righteous fasting during Lent. Joe stopped and asked for God's mercy.

We are all as vulnerable to pride and self-righteousness as the Pharisee in today's gospel passage. The Pharisee separated himself from the others and boasted of his goodness. He asked nothing of God, presuming he wasn't in need of God's mercy. In contrast, the tax collector humbly stood far off and acknowledged his sinfulness. The sinner goes home justified while the "religious" man does not.

ACT

Today I will be mindful of the areas of my life (times of arrogance and judgment) in need of God's mercy. I will pray for forgiveness and the ability to open my heart and mind to these amazing gifts.

PRAY

Compassionate Father, have mercy on me, a sinner. Bless me with the virtue of humility and give me a heart full of mercy, especially for those I find difficult to accept and love. Amen.

Sunday, March 14
Fourth Week of Lent

BEGIN

Spend a minute or two in silence. Put your hand over your heart and listen for the Lord to call your name.

PRAY

For by grace you have been saved through faith, and this is not from you; it is the gift of God.

~Ephesians 2:8

LISTEN

Read John 3:14–21.

For God so loved the world that he gave his only Son, so that everyone who believes in him might not perish but might have eternal life.

~John 3:16

God Is Very Fond of Me

Fr. Edward Farrell tells the story of a priest in the west of Ireland. Out on a walk, he was caught in a downpour and took shelter under a large tree, along with an elderly gentleman. The man took out his rosary beads and was quietly saying his prayers. When the man finished, the priest said, "You're great at the praying." "Ah, yes," the man replied, "God is very fond of me."

I love this story. That man knew in the depths of his being that God loved him in a very personal and familiar way. Sr. Honora, my friend, shared this story with me, and commented, "Our God is not a stingy God—he shares love freely and abundantly." The challenge is to accept and live in this tremendous love.

Every day God is among us, within us, and around us. Yet in Jesus, God sent a unique and incomparably clear sign of his presence. John tells us that God loves the world—this is huge. The "world" in John's gospel refers most often to people who are at odds with Jesus and God. Yet in this passage we are told that the Son did not come to condemn the world but to shed light on it. Our God is rich in mercy. So those who see are invited to participate in God's vision for our world—the "in-breaking" of the reign, or kingdom, of God. Hans Küng, a noted theologian, describes the kingdom of God as "God's creation healed." We are healed and participate in the healing of all creation with Jesus, in both this life and the next.

The God who loves the world is so fond of you, loves you personally, uniquely, and unconditionally. God invites you to friendship through Jesus, who came not to condemn but to set you free.

ACT

Today I will find a quiet space. With my eyes closed, I will say repeatedly, "God is so fond of me."

PRAY

Loving God, thank you for being so fond of me that you sent your Son to reveal your boundless love. Give me the grace to accept the gift of Jesus in my heart so that I may be born anew. Amen.

Monday, March 15
Fourth Week of Lent

BEGIN

Spend a minute or two in silence. Put your hand over your heart and listen for the Lord to call your name.

PRAY

Hear, O Lord, and have pity on me; O Lord, be my helper.

~Psalm 30:10

LISTEN

Read John 4:43–54.

The royal official said to Jesus, "Sir, come down before my child dies." Jesus said to him, "You may go; your son will live." The man believed what Jesus said to him and left.

~John 4:49–50

Please, God

I was watching an episode of the television series *Bob Hearts Abishola* in which Bob, a wealthy Midwestern businessman, falls in love with Abishola, a nurse and traditional Nigerian woman. Undaunted by the vast differences in their backgrounds, Bob is determined to win Abishola's heart. In one episode, Abishola invites Bob to church, but Bob is reluctant and says he doesn't believe in God and all that "woo woo" stuff. Abishola, surprised and insulted, asks him about his prayer in the hospital chapel when his mother was in intensive care. He says, "Oh that. I only pray when it is the last resort." She replies, "But God answered your prayer, your mother recovered." Bob responds, "Oh, I never gave that another thought." For both believers and non-believers, prayer is an instinctive response to a crisis.

The royal official described in the gospel passage, a person in high standing in the court of Herod, walked twenty miles from Capernaum to Cana to beg Jesus, a village carpenter, to heal his son. The man was not a believer but heard of Jesus' healing power and likely came to him as a last resort. He surrenders his pride and begs Jesus to come heal his son. Jesus tells him to return home—his son will live. The man believes Jesus and goes home to find his son alive and well.

Like Bob in the television series, the man could have just forgotten about Jesus and gone on with his life. Yet the scripture passage tells us that the royal official and his whole household believed. This would not have been easy for him as a member of Herod's court. He probably would have had to endure jibes and mockery, and some would have thought he was a bit crazy. Still, the royal official began with a desperate need, experienced Jesus' healing power, and believed. He and his family became faithful followers of Christ.

ACT

I will reflect today on the gift of faith and the many gifts that God has given me and say thanks.

PRAY

Good and gracious God, thank you for the gift of faith. Give me a heart full of gratitude for the many ways you answer my prayers and enrich my life. Strengthen my faith with a deep trust in you. I surrender all my needs and worries into your hands. Amen.

BEGIN

Spend a minute or two in silence. Put your hand over your heart and listen for the Lord to call your name.

PRAY

God is our refuge and our strength, an ever-present help in distress.

~Psalm 46:2

LISTEN

Read John 5:1–16.

Jesus said to him, "Rise, take up your mat, and walk." Immediately the man became well.

~John 5:8–9

She Enjoys Ill Health

"Do you want to get well?" may seem like a silly question. A friend of mind told me that her dad would say, speaking of one of her aunts who was always complaining about her ailments, "She enjoys ill health." It is a great line!

Sometimes complaining of a physical ailment allows us to avoid responsibility or express an emotional ailment. Even when you don't choose to suffer, it is still tough to choose wellness. My sister Mary hated to go to physical therapy after her knee replacement. One day I went with her, and I cringed as they tried to bend her knee to a ninety-degree angle. Therapy hurts. It was tempting for Mary skip therapy and her exercises, but her desire to walk without pain overcame her desire to avoid the pain required to get there. We often know what it takes to be healthy, but we don't always choose it.

In today's gospel passage, the story centers on the paralyzed man. He has waited for thirty-eight years to enter the healing waters. When Jesus asks him if he wants to be well, he doesn't answer. Instead, he blames others for getting ahead of him into the pool. Jesus tells him to rise, pick up his mat, and walk. The man does just that, and his life changes. Change, even good change, is scary. Later in the story, Jesus also forgives this man's sins. The man receives a physical and a spiritual healing, reminding us that our minds, bodies, and spirits are all connected.

The paralyzed man got up that morning, planning to do the same thing he had done for thirty-eight years. He didn't expect that day would be any different from the last. Jesus enters his life, and everything changes. He no longer relies on willpower to move him but instead relies on Jesus, the power of God, to make him physically and spiritually well.

ACT

I will address one area in my life that needs healing and take a single step in that direction today. I will make a timely doctor's appointment, start an exercise plan, research healthy eating, or receive the Sacrament of Reconciliation.

PRAY

Lord Jesus, help me to name any illness, sin, or distress that is paralyzing me. Empower me to do what I need to do to be alive and well. Open my heart to hear you say, "Rise and live!" Amen.

WEDNESDAY, MARCH 17
ST. PATRICK'S FEAST DAY, MEMORIAL
FOURTH WEEK OF LENT

BEGIN

Spend a minute or two in silence. Put your hand over your heart and listen for the Lord to call your name.

PRAY

The Lord is good to all and compassionate toward all his work.

~Psalm 145:9

LISTEN

Read John 5:17–30.

The Son cannot do anything on his own, but only what he sees the Father doing; for what he does the Son will also do.

~John 5:19

St. Patrick: More Than Shamrocks and Green Beer

Today we celebrate the feast day of St. Patrick. Patrick grew up in a devout Christian home, his father a deacon and his grandfather a priest. As a teenager, he was kidnapped from his home in England and was enslaved in Ireland. Separated from his family and homeland, he slowly turned toward God in prayer. He was changed by his newfound relationship with Christ. He eventually escaped Ireland and returned home. One night, he had a dream. He heard a voice calling him to return to Ireland to do the work of God. Patrick struggled with returning to minister to the people who had enslaved him. Courageously, he trusted in God, set sail for Ireland, and brought the Christian faith to thousands. His complete faith and utter dependence on the power of God working in and through him was amazing.

One of St. Patrick's legacies is a prayer attributed to him called The Breastplate. This is a stanza of the prayer translated by Thomas Cahill: "I arise today; through God's strength to pilot me, God's might to uphold me, God's wisdom to guide me, God's eye to look before me, God's ear to hear me, God's word to speak for me, God's hand to guard me, God's way to lie before me, God's shield to protect me, God's host to save me."

In today's gospel passage, Jesus responds to the accusations and concerns of the religious leaders that he was breaking the Sabbath and equating himself with God. He answers them by stating clearly that his work is totally dependent on God. Patrick, too, faced strong opposition when he returned to Ireland, but he placed his trust in God's strength to pilot him and uphold him. As disciples of Christ, we are called to speak God's word of peace and reconciliation despite opposition. We arise each day, entrusting ourselves to the guidance and protection of our God.

ACT

Today I will share in conversation or through social media that St. Patrick is more than shamrocks and green beer. I will offer a bit of the legend about St. Patrick, or the lines of his Breastplate prayer.

PRAY

I arise today through God's strength to pilot me, God's might to uphold me, and God's wisdom to guide me. St. Patrick, pray for me. Amen.

THURSDAY, MARCH 18
FOURTH WEEK OF LENT

BEGIN

Spend a minute or two in silence. Put your hand over your heart and listen for the Lord to call your name.

PRAY

God so loved the world that he gave his only-begotten Son, so that everyone who believes in him might have eternal life.

~John 3:16

LISTEN

Read John 5:31–47.

The Father who sent me has testified on my behalf.

~John 5:37

Dorothy Day: A Witness to God's Work

Dorothy Day, the cofounder of the Catholic Worker Movement, is sometimes described as a modern-day St. Augustine because of her checkered past. Before converting to Catholicism, she had an abortion and a child born out of wedlock, and she had close associations with communists. Yet Dorothy became a devout Catholic and grounded her social activism in the Gospel of Jesus Christ. She had a passion for both intimacy with God and social justice, and she served Christ by serving the poor. She opened houses of hospitality for the poor and was an advocate for the rights of workers, a pacifist, and a strong voice for the dignity of all human life.

In her early days, bishops distanced themselves from her and at least one tried to silence her. Despite her deep faith, the testimony of those who knew her, and her incredible works of charity and justice, some religious leaders did not recognize her as doing God's work. Today, she is on the path toward canonization, and Pope Francis, in his 2015 address to the US Congress, named her one of four exemplary Americans of this century.

In today's gospel passage, Jesus is once again defending himself against the accusations of his opponents. They cannot see the gift of God in Jesus because he does not follow the letter of the law, despite the testimony of God himself, the word of John the Baptist, and Jesus' mighty works of healing and mercy. Still, his opponents refuse to believe he is from God.

God is in our midst and sometimes is revealed to us in people we least expect—people we may disagree with or who challenge our assumptions. We will know them by their works. As followers of Christ, we will also face opposition, but we continue to do works of mercy and acts of kindness. These works are evidence that the power of God is working in and through us.

ACT

As a sign of commitment to Christ, I will do a work of mercy or an act of kindness today.

PRAY

God our Creator, Dorothy Day served Christ by serving the poor and being a voice for the downtrodden. She gave testimony to you through her works of mercy and witness to justice and peace. Inspire me to turn to Christ as my Savior and see his face in the poor and suffering. Dorothy Day, servant of God, pray for me. Amen.

Friday, March 19

Solemnity of St. Joseph, Husband of Mary

Fourth Week of Lent

BEGIN

Spend a minute or two in silence. Put your hand over your heart and listen for the Lord to call your name.

PRAY

The promises of the Lord I will sing forever.

~*Psalm 89:2*

LISTEN

Read Matthew 1:16, 18–21, 24.

It is through the Holy Spirit that this child has been conceived.

~*Matthew 1:20b*

St. Joseph's Table Feeds the Poor and Nourishes the Spirit

The scriptures say little about St. Joseph, Joseph never speaks in the gospels, and yet he is a favorite patron of many Christians. Pope Francis, for example, has a special devotion to St. Joseph and cherishes a statue of Joseph sleeping—or, better, dreaming. Francis has mentioned in various addresses that he places difficult prayer requests under the statue.

Italians celebrate March 19 as both St. Joseph's feast day and Father's Day. One traditional celebration is the St. Joseph table, which originated in Sicily in the Middle Ages. Legend says that Sicily was suffering from a severe drought and Sicilians prayed to St. Joseph for relief. When the rains finally came, the people celebrated with special tables filled with an assortment of food from their harvest. These tables or altars were also decorated with Christian symbols and candles. After thanking St. Joseph, they distributed the food to people in need.

Many parishes in the United States have adopted the tradition of St. Joseph's table. They honor St. Joseph on his feast day by giving thanks to God for all the gifts received and by giving to people who have less. This custom feeds the poor and nourishes the spirit of the entire community. A table is decorated with a statue of Joseph, other religious symbols, and all sorts of delicious bread, foods, and pastries. Usually, there is a blessing of the table and a meal, and the food is donated to people in need in the local area.

St. Joseph is described in the scriptures as just and righteous; there is very little else directly known about him. But what we do know is that he listened to and heeded God's word, he was just in caring for Mary when he found out she was pregnant, and he took care of his family during difficult times. Joseph reminds us to take care of one another and support our families—without condition.

ACT

Today I will create a St. Joseph table at home. I will decorate the table with the help of family or friends, pray together, bless the table, share a meal, or deliver some food to a local food pantry or to a family who may be struggling.

PRAY

St. Joseph, intercede for me and my family. Protect us, unite us, help us to be obedient to God's will and care for one another and our neighbors. St. Joseph, protector of families, pray for us. Amen.

SATURDAY, MARCH 20
FOURTH WEEK OF LENT

BEGIN

Spend a minute or two in silence. Put your hand over your heart and listen for the Lord to call your name.

PRAY

Sustain the just, O searcher of heart and soul, O just God.

~Psalm 7:9b

LISTEN

Read John 7:40–53.

Some in the crowd who heard these words of Jesus said, "This is truly the Prophet."

~John 7:40

God Comes from Unexpected Persons and Places

Nelson Mandela became the first Black president of South Africa after spending twenty-seven years in prison for leading the anti-apartheid movement there. Mandela was born, like Jesus, in a small country village—in Mandela's case, it was Mvezo, South Africa. Who would have believed that an incarcerated, poor Black man from the country would become president of South Africa, a Nobel Prize winner, and a globally recognized civil rights leader?

Mandela won over the hearts and minds of many South Africans and the world. Even his prison guards began to wonder if he was a righteous man and the hope of South Africa. Mandela wrote, "If you talk to a person in a language he understands, that goes to his head. If you talk to him in his language, that goes to his heart." Like Jesus, Mandela spoke the language of the heart.

Many people believed in his message; however, those in positions of power and privilege were slow to accept it.

In today's gospel passage, there are several different reactions to Jesus' message. The officers who were sent to arrest him are amazed and bewildered by the power of his word. The chief priests and Pharisees respond to Jesus and his growing movement with contempt. If he was the Christ, he would not have come from an obscure village like Galilee, they claim. The third response is from Nicodemus, a Pharisee and member of the Sanhedrin. He has been touched by Jesus but gives a timid response in his defense. Nicodemus is likely afraid to take a stand because of obvious repercussions from his cohort of synagogue officials.

We sometimes find ourselves in a position in which we are prompted to defend our faith in Jesus Christ. Sometimes people challenge our membership in the Catholic Church, and others—even Catholics—our adherence to Catholic social teachings. The best way to respond is with your heart and your experience, by explaining, "This is what I believe and why."

ACT

Today I will identify someone I wrote off because of where they come from, their educational background, religion, race, or political party. I will try this week to listen directly to what that person has said or written or make a commitment to listen to news from different ideological perspectives than my own.

PRAY

Jesus, you are the Christ. I recommit to following you wholeheartedly this day. When my faith is challenged and dismissed, give me the grace to share my faith with humility and confidence and always from the heart. Amen.

SUNDAY, MARCH 21
FIFTH WEEK OF LENT

BEGIN

Spend a minute or two in silence. Put your hand over your heart and listen for the Lord to call your name.

PRAY

I will place my law within them and write it upon their hearts; I will be their God and they shall be my people.

~Jeremiah 31:33

LISTEN

Read John 12:20–33.

Whoever loves his life loses it, and whoever hates his life in this world will preserve it for eternal life.

~John 12:25

God Is Bigger than Elvis

In 1963, the young film star Dolores Hart became a Benedictine nun, surprising most people who knew her or followed her career. She had shared the screen with some of the biggest stars of the day, such as Montgomery Clift, Marlon Brando, and Elvis Presley. Her decision to become a nun did not please everyone. Her agent told her that she had "just swallowed a razor blade."

Mother Dolores now has been a nun for more than fifty years and became prioress of her monastery in Connecticut. She recalls that when she entered religious life at twenty-four years of age, she struggled to let go of all her belongings—fur coats, jewels, and dresses. It was a kind of dying. She says that although she had loved her acting career, she found deeper meaning and love in her vocation as a Benedictine sister. "I didn't run away from something, but I ran toward something—new life in Christ."

Those who were angry or simply didn't understand why Dolores would give up "everything" had not grasped the lesson that Jesus teaches in the gospel passage for today: Our faith is about dying so that new life can arise. It is about Jesus dying so that he could overcome both death and sin by emerging from the tomb, and it is about the many deaths each of us must die so that, through our deaths, might come new life. This is the meaning of the sacrifices of Lent—not losing weight or overcoming a smoking habit, beneficial as those outcomes might be, but dying to preoccupation with material things so that we might better discern and act on greater things.

You don't have to give up your career like Mother Dolores, but you should examine the opportunities that God offers you to sacrifice your own will and embrace his will.

ACT

Today I will sort through drawers and closets and find an item in good condition to give away—perhaps one of my prized possessions.

PRAY

Loving God and Father, I stand before you as a seed that must die. I struggle to hold on to my lofty goals and accomplishments and my prized possessions. Yet you teach me that I must lose my very life in order to find my true life. I offer today my yes to do your will as I seek new life in your Son, Jesus. Amen.

MONDAY, MARCH 22
FIFTH WEEK OF LENT

BEGIN

Spend a minute or two in silence. Put your hand over your heart and listen for the Lord to call your name.

PRAY

Even though I walk in the dark valley I fear no evil;
for you are at my side.

~Psalm 23:4ab

LISTEN

Read John 8:1–11.

[Jesus] said to them, "Let the one among you who is without sin be the first to throw a stone at her."

~John 8:7

No One Is Beyond Redemption

A minor character in *Gone with the Wind* is Belle Watling, who runs a prosperous brothel in Atlanta. With the Civil War raging, Belle offers to donate money to a hospital treating wounded Confederate soldiers, but she is rudely rebuffed because of her sinful profession. She offers the money again—through Melanie Hamilton, one of the proper ladies of Atlanta. And Melanie, risking her own reputation, treats Belle respectfully, thanks her for her generosity, and accepts the donation.

Later, when Atlanta has been occupied by federal troops, Belle saves the life of Melanie's husband, Ashley, by lying to Yankee officers about Ashley's whereabouts. Again, Melanie expresses her gratitude for Belle's noble intentions. Melanie did not approve of Belle's livelihood any more than Jesus approved of the adulterous behavior of the woman we read about in today's gospel passage. But in both cases, a rigid and hypocritical social order placed sinful people in a category from which there was no redemption.

No, Jesus says with his treatment of the embarrassed and terrified woman, we must recognize in each other—whatever our flaws and failures—the human dignity we have received from God. We must recognize in each other the potential for good that is present in every soul. We must offer each other the respect and compassion that says, "I do not condemn you." We must not reject people as though Jesus hasn't won the possibility of redemption for all of us. Jesus' last words to the beleaguered woman were, "From now on, do not sin anymore." He was telling her that she could begin again.

Every Lent, we can give ourselves that opportunity to begin again—to get back on the sacred path. We can also desire it and pray for it for others, whoever they may be.

ACT

Today I will do an examination of conscience and receive the Sacrament of Reconciliation before Easter.

PRAY

Merciful God, thank you for always giving me another chance to begin again. Forgive my sins and help me not to sin anymore. I pray for those I love who have separated themselves from your will and way. Show them your mercy and help me to be patient with them. Amen.

TUESDAY, MARCH 23
FIFTH WEEK OF LENT

BEGIN

Spend a minute or two in silence. Put your hand over your heart and listen for the Lord to call your name.

PRAY

O LORD, hear my prayer, and let my cry come to you.
Hide not your face from me in the day of my distress.

~Psalm 102:2–3

LISTEN

Read John 8:21–30.

The one who sent me is with me. He has not left me alone, because I always do what is pleasing to him.

~John 8:29

Look to the Cross and Live

One Lent, I was giving a parish retreat in West Texas with one of my Dominican brothers. It was my first time in that part of the country. I was taken aback by a big billboard advertising a rattlesnake roundup. These amazing events draw tens of thousands of people, and they are great fundraisers for local charities. During the roundups, snakes are milked of their venom, which is collected for medical research—even rattlesnakes have a positive side.

In today's first reading from the book of Numbers, snakes are having a roundup in the middle of the Israelite desert camp. There were many detours and delays on the Israelites' journey to the Promised Land, and understandably, the people became cranky again. However, this time their complaints were not only against Moses but also against God. God responded by sending them a plague of snakes. Many were bitten and died. The people confessed their sin, and Moses prayed on their behalf. God listened and instructed Moses to make a serpent out of bronze and mount it on a pole. Any victim of snake-bites who looked at the bronze serpent would live. The Israelites had confessed their sin earlier on the journey and went right back to sinning against God. This time God gave them an ongoing reminder that each person needs to turn to the healing power of God.

In the gospel passage today, when Jesus refers to the Son of Man being "lifted up," he is making a connection to the well-known image of the snake being lifted on the pole in the desert. The pole in John's gospel, like the pole with the bronze serpent, means both the poison of death and the life-giving power of God for all those who believe. As we approach Holy Week, we are invited to stand before the Cross in our brokenness and look to Christ for healing and new life. Jesus is the I AM, the unique revelation of God in our human story.

ACT

Today I will research Good Friday liturgies in my area and start rearranging my schedule as needed to attend one.

PRAY

Suffering Christ, you are the I AM. Strengthen my belief in your redeeming work on the Cross. I turn from my sinful ways and turn toward you. I gaze upon your Cross looking for healing and new life. Amen.

WEDNESDAY, MARCH 24
FIFTH WEEK OF LENT

BEGIN

Spend a minute or two in silence. Put your hand over your heart and listen for the Lord to call your name.

PRAY

Blessed are they who have kept the word with a generous heart and yield a harvest through perseverance.

~Luke 8:15

LISTEN

Read John 8:31–42.

If you remain in my word, you will truly be my disciples, and you will know the truth, and the truth will set you free.

~John 8:31–32

Truth: Let's Google It

My niece Kate was reading the Christmas story to her precocious seven-year-old son, Andrew. When she got to the part about Mary and Joseph being turned away from the inn, Andrew stopped her. He said, "Wait just one minute. That can't be true." Kate replied, "Yes, Andrew, that is the truth." He said, "No way, Mom. Let's Google it."

No, Andrew, Google doesn't know everything, and what it does "know" is sometimes not the truth. We now have access to more information than ever, but that also means that we have access to more *inaccurate* information, so we must be sure of the source. Seeking the truth has always been hard work but may be more so in our current information age.

Catholics must recover the practice of seeking truth. For me, one way is to refrain from believing everything I read on the web or sharing things I don't know to be true. I think it is particularly harmful and sinful when we circulate misinformation and slander on social media, whether we realize it or not. When we are not rigorous in seeking truth and checking sources, we can easily spread false news. Other times we assume something is false news because we don't agree with it. I am shocked and dismayed at what Catholics will circulate about other Catholics with whom they don't agree.

In today's gospel passage, Jesus makes three promises to those who commit to obey his word: They will be his disciples, they will know the truth, and the truth will set them free. Where our faith is concerned, there is only one source of truth: the Word of God. The Word calls us to treat every person with dignity, mercy, and justice—and that is not false news.

ACT

I will make a commitment today to check the source of a story before spreading it by word of mouth or on social media. If it is something negative about someone, I will choose not to share it, even if it is true.

PRAY

Jesus, you are the way, the truth, and the life. Help me to be obedient to your word and recover the practice of truth as a way of life. Set me free by the truth of your love and your call to love my neighbor as myself. Amen.

Thursday, March 25

Solemnity of the Annunciation of the Lord

Fifth Week of Lent

BEGIN

Spend a minute or two in silence. Put your hand over your heart and listen for the Lord to call your name.

PRAY

To do your will, O my God, is my delight, and your law is within my heart.

~Psalm 40:8

LISTEN

Read Luke 1:26–38.

Behold, I am the handmaid of the Lord. May it be done to me according to your word.

~Luke 1:38a

Mary, the Air We Breathe

Gerard Manley Hopkins, a Jesuit poet, wrote the poem "The Blessed Virgin Compared to the Air We Breathe." He wrote the poem in May of 1883 to be hung near the statue of the Blessed Mother in his Jesuit residence to celebrate the month of Mary. The first two lines of the poem are my favorites:

Wild air, world-mothering air,
Nestling me everywhere.

Hopkins maintains that just as the air and the sun's energy sustain our physical life, so too Mary sustains our spiritual life and mediates our relationship with God. Hopkins invites us to breathe Mary, in order to breathe more Christ, the mercy of God.

The angel Gabriel makes a staggering announcement to Mary: She will have a baby, and he will be the Son of God. Mary is perplexed, to say the least. She asks, "How can this be?" She is troubled and ponders the message of the angel—she takes it all in. Then she steps into the unknown with faith and courage and says a resounding yes to God. God is incarnated into Mary's very being and she brings forth God to the world. Mary inhales the Spirit of God and exhales Jesus, the mercy of God. Her wild, *world-mothering air* which nestled Jesus also nestles us. She beckons us to breathe in Jesus and breathe out his mercy to our wounded world.

ACT

I will search for the full poem by Gerard Manley Hopkins, read it slowly, and identify a line that speaks to my heart. On this Solemnity of the Annunciation, I will share this phrase on social media or with a friend.

PRAY

Hail Mary, mother of Jesus, surround me with your *world-mothering air*. Hail Mary, pray for me that I may breathe in your Son, Jesus, and breathe out his mercy to our wounded world. Hail Mary, full of grace, pray for me so that I may say yes in faith to God's call. Amen.

Friday, March 26
Fifth Week of Lent

BEGIN

Spend a minute or two in silence. Put your hand over your heart and listen for the Lord to call your name.

PRAY

In my distress I called upon the LORD and cried out to my God; From his temple he heard my voice, and my cry to him reached his ears.

~Psalm 18:7

LISTEN

Read John 10:31–42.

If I do not perform my Father's works, do not believe me; but if I perform them, even if you do not believe me, believe the works, so that you may realize and understand that the Father is in me and I am in the Father.

~John 10:37–38

God's Works amid the Coronavirus Pandemic

During the coronavirus pandemic, with all the fear and self-concern, people were still doing God's work. One friend was getting out of her car in the parking lot of the supermarket when an elderly couple called to her from their car window. They asked her if she would take their $40 and their shopping list and pick up some groceries. They were terrified to enter the crowded store and possibly catch the virus. My friend reassured them and gladly picked up their items, offering to deliver groceries to their home in the future. A couple of kids knew an elderly neighbor lived alone and was sheltering in place. To her delight, they performed a cello concert on her patio. A local dance studio blasted music on the lawn in front of a seniors' residence, and kids—six feet apart— were dancing. Residents called to them and clapped from their windows. Health-care workers, doctors, nurses, home attendants, husbands, wives, and friends risked their health and cared for the rest of us. All over the world, people helped their neighbors in new ways amid the pandemic.

Like Jesus, God is in us and we are in God. Jesus worked many miracles when he walked the earth. He healed the sick, transformed lives, and even raised the dead. However, even when the religious authorities witnessed these mighty works, they did not believe. Yet Jesus kept inviting them to follow him. Signs of God's works are all around us. Jesus continues to do his work today through the hands and hearts of ordinary people. Some cynics are suspicious of people who do good works. There are doomsayers who have no faith in God nor in humanity. But, like Jesus, we continue to do the work of our God without looking for approval or reward. As Jesus revealed God, we are called to reveal Jesus to the world by charitable works and just acts.

ACT

Today I will do a work of God for someone in need.

PRAY

God of the ill and brokenhearted, give me the grace to reveal Jesus today by my loving words and kind actions. Help me to show others that I care about them. Amen.

Saturday, March 27
Fifth Week of Lent

BEGIN

Spend a minute or two in silence. Put your hand over your heart and listen for the Lord to call your name.

PRAY

My dwelling shall be with them; I will be their God, and they shall be my people.

~Ezekiel 37:27

LISTEN

Read John 11:45–56.

Caiaphas, who was high priest that year, said to them, "You know nothing, nor do you consider that it is better for you that one man should die instead of the people, so that the whole nation may not perish."

~John 11:49–50

Greed Quenched a Heroic Life

In *Creation at the Crossroads*, a RENEW small-group book about saving the environment, Fr. Edward Ciuba tells the story of Sr. Dorothy Stang, S.N.D., an American missionary. In 1966, she went to Coroatá, Brazil, and soon became a champion of farmers who were being driven off their land by powerful ranchers. She also became an advocate for indigenous groups and the forest itself. The ranchers were ravaging the land, destroying the Amazon region for increased profit. Very often, they paid off police and judges to have their way. Sr. Dorothy would protest outside police stations and courthouses, demanding that the rights of the people be upheld. The ranchers put a $50,000 bounty on her head—better that one woman die so that the powerful and wealthy would not be inconvenienced. Sr. Dorothy, seventy-three years old, was killed after a meeting of ranchers, and her body was left alongside a muddy road. Yet her death brought greater attention to the ranchers and her sacrifice encouraged people of that area to continue her cries for justice.

After Jesus raises Lazarus from dead, the crowds begin to follow him. This forces the hand of the Jewish authorities. They feared that Jesus' movement would raise a disturbance against the Roman government. If the authorities could not control Jesus followers, the Romans might come and take away their power and privilege. The Jewish authorities do not seek the truth about Jesus, and they never consider that he may be the Messiah. They are too worried about how Jesus could affect their careers, land, and nation. They decide to eliminate Jesus, but his death does not save them. In AD 70, the Romans destroy Jerusalem and the Temple.

Like Jesus, Sr. Dorothy gave her life freely for the world. We are inspired by her heroic witness to place doing the right thing over our own careers and prosperity and work together for the common good.

ACT

I will research the life of Sr. Dorothy Stang today and learn more about the continuing struggle to save the local farmers and the Amazon for the common good.

PRAY

Lord Jesus, Savior of the world, as I prepare to walk with you during Holy Week, give me a courageous and expansive heart that is ready and willing to take a risk and to give my life away for the sake of the common good. Amen.

SUNDAY, MARCH 28
PALM SUNDAY OF THE LORD'S PASSION

BEGIN

Spend a minute or two in silence. Put your hand over your heart and listen for the Lord to call your name.

PRAY

[Christ] humbled himself, becoming obedient to the point of death, even death on a cross.

~Philippians 2:8

LISTEN

Read Mark 11:1–10.

They brought the colt to Jesus and put their cloaks over it. And he sat on it.

~Mark 11:7

The Donkey

In my parish, Our Lady of Peace, in New Providence, New Jersey, a donkey leads the Palm Sunday procession from the parking lot to the entrance of the church. The donkey brings lots of excitement, especially to the children, and it offers a new energy to the liturgy.

We enter the Church and join the full congregation in singing "Hosanna" and waving palm branches. (The donkey stays outside.) The mood is high until the Mass readings begin and we solemnly participate in the Passion dialogue. It is a sobering reminder that some of the people who cry "Hosanna" and wave palm leaves are the ones who cry "Crucify him" a few days later. We begin the liturgy with *Hooray! Here comes Jesus!* and by the end of the service we nail Jesus to the Cross.

We all have a place in Palm Sunday. We could be the people cheering, "Hosanna! Blessed is he who comes in the name of the Lord," and who later betray or deny him or even call for his Crucifixion. Maybe we are all these characters at different times and in varying degrees in our lives. As I reflect on all the characters in the Palm Sunday narrative, I think I would prefer to be the donkey, set free to accompany and serve Christ—a jackass for Jesus.

Jesus suffered and died because of the sins of the world. Mark's account of the Passion ends with the body of Jesus being sealed in a tomb, but the story doesn't end there. Our entrance into Holy Week points us toward Easter and the joy it promises. We accompany Jesus and one another through the suffering of this week in the firm belief that in the outpouring of Jesus' life we receive not only the gift of salvation but also the giver of the gift as well. On Easter, we celebrate the truth that we will rise again with Jesus in this life and in the next.

ACT

Today I will make plans to attend an additional Holy Week service at a local parish.

PRAY

Jesus, my Lord and my Savior, help me to experience your love in a more profound way as I enter Holy Week and reflect on your Passion, Death, and Resurrection. Let your Holy Spirit flood my heart that I may be open to new invitations to die and rise again for the life of the world. Amen.

MONDAY, MARCH 29
HOLY WEEK

BEGIN

Spend a minute or two in silence. Put your hand over your heart and listen for the Lord to call your name.

PRAY

The LORD is my light and my salvation; whom should I fear?

~Psalm 27:1

LISTEN

Read John 12:1–11.

Mary took a liter of costly perfumed oil made from genuine aromatic nard and anointed the feet of Jesus and dried them with her hair.

~John 12:3

Waste Love, Not Food

My dad grew up during the Great Depression and World War II, and the lack of food and need for rationing left an indelible mark on him. He would often remind us to clean our plates and not waste food because there were hungry children in Africa. I would have gladly given those kids my lima beans but wondered if they would really want them. No, a child cleaning her plate will not stop children in poorer circumstances from being hungry, but lessons about not wasting food and having concern for those who are food insecure *are* important.

According to the US Department of Agriculture, in the United States alone, food waste is estimated at between 30 and 40 percent of the food supply. This same pattern can be found worldwide. Food that spoils in supermarkets or gets scraped into the garbage in homes and restaurants is truly wasted. But in the gospel passage for this day, what Mary did with the expensive oil was not a waste. This kind of oil was often used by wealthy people as perfumes. Mary used the oil in an act of worshipping the Christ, which was a far more fitting use than personal adornment.

Mary did not just sprinkle oil on Jesus but broke the jar and anointed him with the full contents. She generously "wasted" her perfumed oil on Jesus. Love and mercy flowed between them. Judas and some of the others accused her of being wasteful while Jesus knew her heart and accepted her gift as a healing balm. How he must have needed the strength of that love as he prepared for the suffering he was about to face.

Many times, we think of doing a kind act for someone but never do it. It may be because we feel awkward about it or because we get busy and put the thoughtful action aside. If love is true, there must be a certain extravagance to it. We waste love only when we are stingy with it.

ACT

I will perform a kind and loving gesture, however small, today.

PRAY

Good and gracious God, open my heart to accept the love you lavish upon me. Give me a generous spirit so I may share your love with all those you have placed in my life. Amen.

Tuesday, March 30
Holy Week

BEGIN

Spend a minute or two in silence. Put your hand over your heart and listen for the Lord to call your name.

PRAY

In you, O Lord, I take refuge; let me never be put to shame.

~Psalm 71:1

LISTEN

Read John 13:21–33, 36–38.

Reclining at table with his disciples, Jesus was deeply troubled and testified, "Amen, amen, I say to you, one of you will betray me."

~John 13:21

Small Stuff Matters

Benedict Arnold, an American general, was once a revered hero in the American Revolution. He later betrayed his fellow revolutionaries and went over to the British. As a result, his name has become synonymous with "treason" and "betrayal," just as the name of Judas has. These two men committed betrayal in spectacular ways and are remembered for that. Our challenge is to avoid betraying Jesus even in small ways that only we may know about, but are betrayals nevertheless.

I don't know much about Benedict Arnold's personal life, but I am sure there were a series of small choices that led up to his big betrayal. We know from the biblical accounts that Judas was the disciples' treasurer and that he was regularly stealing small amounts of money collected for the poor (see John 12:6). Many small decisions can often lead to big changes for good or for bad—small stuff matters.

In John's account, Judas and Jesus were seated close by at the table and could speak privately. Another sign of Judas's special relationship with Jesus was that Jesus shared a special bit of food with him. When we are betrayed by such a close friend, the pain is deep. Again and again, Jesus showed his affection toward Judas but was rebuffed. The scripture passage says that Judas left at once—"and it was night." In John's gospel, it is always in darkness that people turn their backs on Christ.

Every time we sin, we choose the darkness and betray Christ. Every time we neglect or mistreat our neighbor, we choose the darkness and betray Christ. We are challenged today to recognize and acknowledge our small betrayals of Christ's love and bring them to the light of God's forgiveness.

ACT

Tonight I will do a brief examination of conscience. I will review the day, thinking about how God has blessed me, give thanks, and then examine ways in which I have sinned—all the times that I have missed the mark in loving God and my neighbor. I will pray for forgiveness.

PRAY

O God, author and source of all light, shine the light of Christ's mercy upon me. Dispel the darkness of doubt, confusion, and fear from my heart. I bring my small betrayals into the light of your love. Thank you for the gift of forgiveness and new life. Amen.

WEDNESDAY, MARCH 31
HOLY WEEK

BEGIN

Spend a minute or two in silence. Put your hand over your heart and listen for the Lord to call your name.

PRAY

I will praise the name of God in song, and I will glorify him with thanksgiving.

~Psalm 69:31

LISTEN

Read Matthew 26:14–25.

The disciples then did as Jesus had ordered and prepared the Passover. When it was evening, he reclined at table with the Twelve.

~Matthew 26:19–20

Kitchen Table

When I was growing up, the kitchen table was the heart of our home. We shared meals and stories, fought over the last piece of chicken, teased and argued. It was in this loud and lively table fellowship that I experienced the bond of family. As I became an adult, it was the place I returned to for conversations with my mom over a cup of tea. At the convent I share with two other sisters, the kitchen table is where we share prayer, food, and life. My favorite thing to do is to share a meal with friends or family.

The Church reminds us that the family is called to be a domestic church—a church in microcosm, a small community of holiness, sacrifice, and service. The domestic church is present in the rough and tumble of family life as it is genuinely lived, not as we might idealize it. The kitchen table is the domestic church's altar—a place we gather to experience communion.

Jesus came with his disciples to Jerusalem to celebrate the Passover meal, a joyous spring festival. He sent them ahead to prepare the place where they would eat the Seder—the Passover meal. Throughout the gospels, we find Jesus at the table with his disciples and friends. In the gospel readings for today and tomorrow, Jesus is gathered with his disciples at the Last Supper. Today is the last full day of Lent. On Holy Thursday, tomorrow at sundown, we celebrate the Lord's Supper, and the meal continues with the washing of the feet and the institution of the Eucharist.

We are called to make our homes holy as we gather around our tables to share prayers of thanksgiving, good food and drink, and meaningful conversation. Easter is a great time to prepare your table, make special foods with love, and gather with friends and family.

ACT

Today and tomorrow are important days of preparation for Easter. I will prepare generously and freely my heart, mind, and home for the Easter celebration.

PRAY

Loving God, lead me into the Triduum with an open heart and a seeking spirit. Help me to prepare for the celebration of Easter with my family and friends joyfully and generously. Amen.

In order to spend time focusing on the Church's services during these holiest of days, the following reflections are shorter than previous days.

THURSDAY, APRIL 1
HOLY THURSDAY

LISTEN

Read John 13:1–15.

I have given you a model to follow, so that as I have done for you, you should also do.

~ John 13:15

Dirty Feet

Since the first Holy Thursday after Pope Francis was inaugurated, he has changed the ritual of washing feet—and shocked the world. Traditionally, popes washed the feet of twelve priests during a solemn Mass in the Basilica of St. John Lateran. Pope Francis has left that tradition behind and moved the ritual to a juvenile detention center, a home for the seriously ill, a center for asylum seekers, and a prison. Francis continues to bring the papacy and the Church closer to the poor and the marginalized. Just as Jesus shocked his disciples by washing their feet, so Francis shocked the world by washing the feet of the least among us.

In Jesus' time, most people wore sandals and the roads were dusty. It was common to provide a basin of water for visitors to wash their feet. If the host was wealthy, a servant would wash the guest's feet. What shocked the disciples was not that someone was washing their feet but that it was Jesus, their teacher and master. They could not believe what Jesus was doing. Jesus' message was clear: Go forth and wash one another's feet.

Jesus, the compassion of God, models for us what it means to be his disciple—a servant. We who partake in the Bread of Life and drink from the cup of salvation are to be Jesus for our world.

ACT

If I am unable to attend Holy Thursday Mass, I will do an act of service for a person in need.

Friday, April 2
Good Friday

LISTEN

Read John 18:1–19:42.

> Jesus said to his mother, "Woman, behold, your son." Then he said to the disciple, "Behold, your mother."
>
> ~*John 19:26*

Women: Faithful to the End

My youngest brother, Peter, was born sixteen months after me, and we spent most of our youth together. When Peter was fifty-nine years old, he was diagnosed with fourth stage esophageal cancer. He was in the prime of his life. His new business was taking off, the last of his three daughters had just gotten married, he had four grandchildren, and loved being the girls' varsity basketball coach at a local high school.

He fought the good fight with his wife, Sally, and his three daughters at his side. All four of them were faithful to him until the end. It is difficult to accompany someone you love who is suffering, but that experience also can transform us. When we look pain and death squarely in the face, we find the courage and strength to carry our loved one into the arms of our loving God.

In all four gospel accounts of the Passion, it is women who keep vigil at Jesus' death. Jesus predicted that all his followers would abandon him, but the women stood firm. They accompanied Jesus in his suffering and found courage when most of the other disciples hid in fear. Mary and the other women who stayed faithful to Jesus in his most difficult hour model what it means to be a disciple: to serve, to love one another, and to share in Jesus' suffering and death.

The cross of suffering leads to new life. The chains of sin and death are broken, and the mystery of death is conquered by Christ's redeeming love. Love is stronger than death.

ACT

Today I will attend the Good Friday Liturgy or take some time to reflect on the Cross and the great love of Christ.

SATURDAY, APRIL 3
HOLY SATURDAY, EASTER VIGIL

LISTEN

Read Mark 16:1–7.

Do not be amazed! You seek Jesus of Nazareth, the crucified. He has been raised; he is not here.

~Mark 16:6

Abandoned by her addict mother, Christine, who was born with multiple disabilities, spent her first two and a half years in hospitals. Eventually she was released to her grandmother's custody and was put in a locked room and ignored. Christine became totally nonresponsive, locked away in her own world. When she was almost three years old, she was placed in foster care. Sr. Ursula, who became her advocate, looked into Christine's beautiful eyes and saw a child of God—full of promise and potential. Sr. Ursula made sure that Christine was placed in a loving home. Her foster parents loved her unconditionally and nurtured her. She began to speak and interact with her new family, and her spirit was gradually released and healed.

During this Easter season, we hear about the power of the Holy Spirit and the faithfulness of the Father's love bring Jesus to new life. The tomb couldn't hold Jesus back, nor should we. It is time to unlock the door, open our hearts, and allow the risen Lord to release our spirits and usher in new life. It is a new moment for us, a resurrection opportunity. Now we can bury the past; it's over, it's forgiven.

Because the tomb is empty, Jesus is alive, Jesus is with us now.

ACT

Today I will reflect on one thing holding me back from living a full life and ask the Lord to release me.

SUNDAY, APRIL 4
EASTER SUNDAY

LISTEN

Read John 20:1–9.

The other disciple also went in, the one who had arrived at the tomb first, and he saw and believed.

~John 20:8

Hope Will Not Be Canceled

Last year, during the Lenten season, we were overwhelmed by the COVID-19 virus. It was a time of fear, uncertainty, and isolation. Almost everything was canceled or made a virtual event, but hope refused to be canceled. People rose above the fear and turned to help their neighbors. Our technologically challenged Church came alive by offering live-streamed Masses, retreats, and Stations of the Cross. Some neighbors turned to chalk art to share messages of hope. One of my favorites was "Hope will not be canceled."

We did not have in-person Easter Sunday Mass or our usual gatherings with family, but Easter nevertheless came, reminding us again that Jesus has defeated death and revealed his merciful love to us. Our Christian faith assures us of the final victory of good over evil, health over sickness, and life over death. Our hope lies in our faith in Jesus Christ and his power to redeem us. As John did, in today's gospel passage, we believe, and because we believe we have hope even in the darkest moments of our lives. Jesus is alive and among us. Amen. Alleluia!

ACT

I will share a sign of hope with someone today.